My Bilingual Picture Book
Moje dvojjazyčná obrázková kniha

Sefa's most beautiful children's stories in one volume

Ulrich Renz • Barbara Brinkmann:

Sleep Tight, Little Wolf · Sladce spi, malý vlku

For ages 2 and up

Cornelia Haas • Ulrich Renz:

My Most Beautiful Dream · Můj nejkrásnější sen

For ages 2 and up

Ulrich Renz • Marc Robitzky:

The Wild Swans · Divoké labutě

Based on a fairy tale by Hans Christian Andersen

For ages 5 and up

© 2024 by Sefa Verlag Kirsten Bödeker, Lübeck, Germany. www.sefa-verlag.de

Special thanks to Paul Bödeker, Freiburg, Germany

All rights reserved.

ISBN: 9783756304295

Read · Listen · Understand

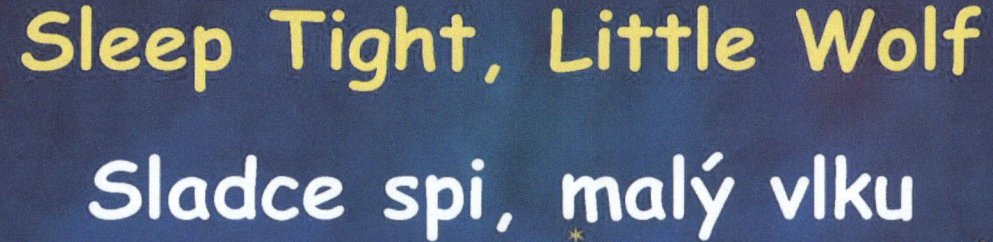

Sleep Tight, Little Wolf
Sladce spi, malý vlku

Ulrich Renz / Barbara Brinkmann

English — bilingual — Czech

Translation:

Pete Savill (English)

Jan Holec (Czech)

Audiobook and video:

www.sefa-bilingual.com/bonus

Password for free access:

English: **LWEN1423**

Czech: **LWCS1228**

Good night, Tim! We'll continue searching tomorrow.
Now sleep tight!

Dobrou noc, Time! Budeme pokračovat v hledání zítra.
Teď se hezky vyspi!

It is already dark outside.

Už je venku tma.

What is Tim doing?

Co tam Tim dělá?

He is leaving for the playground.
What is he looking for there?

Odchází ven na hřiště.
Copak tam hledá?

The little wolf!

He can't sleep without it.

Malého vlka!

Nemůže bez něj spát.

Who's this coming?

Kdo to přichází?

Marie! She's looking for her ball.

Marie! Hledá svůj míč.

And what is Tobi looking for?

A co hledá Tobi?

His digger.

Svůj bagr.

And what is Nala looking for?

A co hledá Nala?

Her doll.

Svou panenku.

Don't the children have to go to bed?

The cat is rather surprised.

Nemusejí jít děti do postele?

Kočka se diví.

Who's coming now?

Kdo přichází teď?

Tim's mum and dad!
They can't sleep without their Tim.

Timova máma a táta.
Bez svého Tima nemůžou spát.

More of them are coming! Marie's dad.
Tobi's grandpa. And Nala's mum.

Přichází jich více! Mariin táta.
Tobiho dědeček. A Nalina máma.

Now hurry to bed everyone!

Teď ale rychle do postele.

Good night, Tim!

Tomorrow we won't have to search any longer.

Dobrou noc Time!

Zítra nebudeme muset hledat déle.

Sleep tight, little wolf!

Sladce spi, malý vlku!

Cornelia Haas • Ulrich Renz

My Most Beautiful Dream
Můj nejkrásnější sen

Translation:

Sefâ Jesse Konuk Agnew (English)

Kateřina Fuková (Czech)

Audiobook and video:

www.sefa-bilingual.com/bonus

Password for free access:

English: **BDEN1423**

Czech: **BDCS1228**

My Most Beautiful Dream
Můj nejkrásnější sen

Cornelia Haas · Ulrich Renz

English — bilingual — Czech

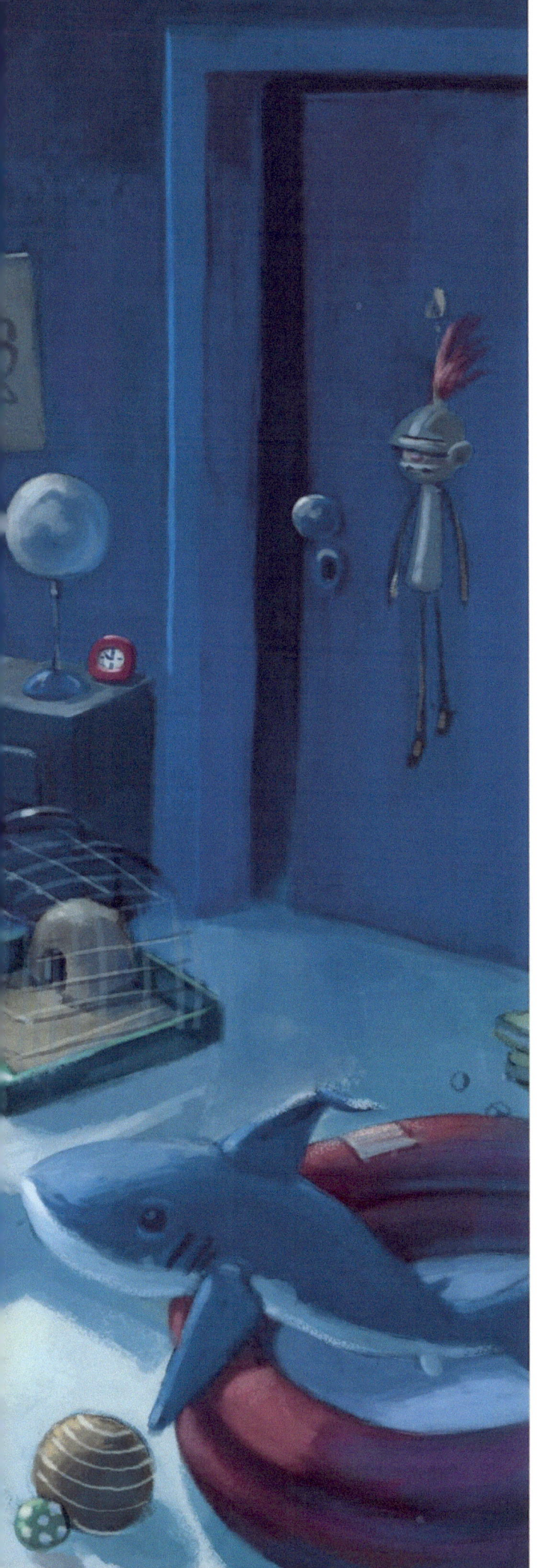

Lulu can't fall asleep. Everyone else is dreaming already – the shark, the elephant, the little mouse, the dragon, the kangaroo, the knight, the monkey, the pilot. And the lion cub. Even the bear has trouble keeping his eyes open …

Hey bear, will you take me along into your dream?

Lulu nemůže usnout. Všichni ostatní už dávno sní – žralok, slon, myška, drak, klokanice, rytíř, opička, pilot. A lvíče. I medvědovi už se zavírají víčka…

Ty medvěde, vezmeš mě do svého snu?

And with that, Lulu finds herself in bear dreamland. The bear catches fish in Lake Tagayumi. And Lulu wonders, who could be living up there in the trees?

When the dream is over, Lulu wants to go on another adventure. Come along, let's visit the shark! What could he be dreaming?

A hned je Lulu v medvědí zemi snů. Medvěd loví ryby v Tagayumiském jezeře. A Lulu si říká, kdo asi bydlí tam vysoko ve stromech?

Sen už končí a Lulu chce na další dobrodružství. Pojď se mnou, navštívíme žraloka! O čem se mu asi zdá?

The shark plays tag with the fish. Finally he's got some friends! Nobody's afraid of his sharp teeth.

When the dream is over, Lulu wants to go on another adventure. Come along, let's visit the elephant! What could he be dreaming?

Žralok hraje s rybami na honěnou. Konečně má nějaké kamarády! Nikdo se už jeho ostrých zubů nebojí.
Sen už končí a Lulu chce na další dobrodružství. Pojďte, navštívíme slona! O čem se mu asi zdá?

The elephant is as light as a feather and can fly! He's about to land on the celestial meadow.

When the dream is over, Lulu wants to go on another adventure. Come along, let's visit the little mouse! What could she be dreaming?

Slon je lehký jako pírko a umí létat! Zrovna přistává na nebeské louce.
Sen už končí a Lulu chce na další dobrodružství. Pojďte, navštívíme myšku!
O čem se jí asi zdá?

The little mouse watches the fair. She likes the roller coaster best. When the dream is over, Lulu wants to go on another adventure. Come along, let's visit the dragon! What could she be dreaming?

Myška sleduje pouť. Nejvíc se jí líbí horská dráha.
Sen už končí a Lulu chce na další dobrodružství. Pojďte, navštívíme draka!
O čem se mu asi zdá?

The dragon is thirsty from spitting fire. She'd like to drink up the whole lemonade lake.

When the dream is over, Lulu wants to go on another adventure. Come along, let's visit the kangaroo! What could she be dreaming?

Drak je žíznivý, protože moc chrlil oheň. Chtěl by vypít celé limonádové jezero.
Sen už končí a Lulu chce na další dobrodružství. Pojďte, navštívíme klokanici! O čem se jí asi zdá?

The kangaroo jumps around the candy factory and fills her pouch. Even more of the blue sweets! And more lollipops! And chocolate!

When the dream is over, Lulu wants to go on another adventure. Come along, let's visit the knight! What could he be dreaming?

Klokanice poskakuje po továrně na sladkosti a plní svůj vak. Ještě více modrých sladkůstek! Ještě více lízátek! A čokolády!

Sen už končí a Lulu chce na další dobrodružství. Pojďte, navštívíme rytíře! O čem se mu asi zdá?

The knight is having a cake fight with his dream princess. Oops! The whipped cream cake has gone the wrong way!

When the dream is over, Lulu wants to go on another adventure. Come along, let's visit the monkey! What could he be dreaming?

Rytíř a jeho vysněná princezna po sobě z legrace hází dorty. Aj! Šlehačkový dort minul cíl.
Sen už končí a Lulu chce na další dobrodružství. Pojďte, navštívíme opičku!
O čem se jí asi zdá?

Snow has finally fallen in Monkeyland. The whole barrel of monkeys is beside itself and getting up to monkey business.
When the dream is over, Lulu wants to go on another adventure. Come along, let's visit the pilot! In which dream could he have landed?

V opičí zemi konečně nasněžilo. Celá opičí tlupa je nadšená a dělá opičárny.

Sen už končí a Lulu chce na další dobrodružství. Pojďte, navštívíme pilota!

V jakém snu asi přistál?

The pilot flies on and on. To the ends of the earth, and even farther, right on up to the stars. No other pilot has ever managed that.
When the dream is over, everybody is very tired and doesn't feel like going on many adventures anymore. But they'd still like to visit the lion cub.
What could she be dreaming?

Pilot letí a letí. Až na kraj země a ještě výš, přímo ke hvězdám. Žádný pilot ještě nedoletěl tak daleko.

Sen už končí a všichni jsou velice unavení. Nikomu se již nechce na další dobrodružství. Chtěli by ale ještě navštívit lvíče. O čem se mu asi zdá?

The lion cub is homesick and wants to go back to the warm, cozy bed.
And so do the others.

And thus begins ...

Lvíčeti se stýská po domově a chce zpět do teplé, útulné postýlky.
A jeho kamarádi to vidí stejně.

A tak začíná ...

... Lulu's
most beautiful dream.

... Lulin nejkrásnější sen.

Ulrich Renz • Marc Robitzky

The Wild Swans

Divoké labutě

Translation:

Ludwig Blohm, Pete Savill (English)

Kateřina Fuková (Czech)

Audiobook and video:

www.sefa-bilingual.com/bonus

Password for free access:

English: **WSEN1423**

Czech: **WSCS1228**

Ulrich Renz · Marc Robitzky

The Wild Swans

Divoké labutě

Based on a fairy tale by

Hans Christian Andersen

English · bilingual · Czech

Once upon a time there were twelve royal children – eleven brothers and one older sister, Elisa. They lived happily in a beautiful castle.

Bylo nebylo dvanáct královských dětí – jedenáct bratrů a jejich starší sestra, Elisa. Šťastně spolu žili v jednom krásném zámku.

One day the mother died, and some time later the king married again. The new wife, however, was an evil witch. She turned the eleven princes into swans and sent them far away to a distant land beyond the large forest.

Jednoho dne jejich matka zemřela a o nějakou dobu později se král znovu oženil. Jeho nová manželka ale byla zlá čarodějka. Zaklela jedenáct princů do labutí a poslala je daleko do země za velkým lesem.

She dressed the girl in rags and smeared an ointment onto her face that turned her so ugly, that even her own father no longer recognized her and chased her out of the castle. Elisa ran into the dark forest.

Princeznu oblékla do otrhaných šatů a pomazala jí obličej tak ošklivou mastí, že ji ani vlastní otec nepoznal a vyhnal ji ze zámku. Elisa utekla do temného lesa.

Now she was all alone, and longed for her missing brothers from the depths of her soul. As the evening came, she made herself a bed of moss under the trees.

Najednou byla úplně sama a z hloubky duše toužila být se svými ztracenými bratry. Když přišel večer, ustlala si postýlku na mechu pod stromy.

The next morning she came to a calm lake and was shocked when she saw her reflection in it. But once she had washed, she was the most beautiful princess under the sun.

Ráno princezna objevila tiché jezero a moc se vyděsila, když na hladině spatřila svůj odraz. Jak se ale umyla vodou, byla nejkrásnějším královským dítětem pod sluncem.

After many days Elisa reached the great sea. Eleven swan feathers were bobbing on the waves.

Po mnoha dnech došla Elisa k širému moři. Na vlnách se pohupovalo jedenáct labutích per.

As the sun set, there was a swooshing noise in the air and eleven wild swans landed on the water. Elisa immediately recognized her enchanted brothers. They spoke swan language and because of this she could not understand them.

Když zapadlo slunce, vzduchem se roznesl svist a na vodě přistálo jedenáct divokých labutí. Elisa ihned poznala své začarované bratry. Protože ale mluvili jen labutí řečí, nerozuměla jim.

During the day the swans flew away, and at night the siblings snuggled up together in a cave.

One night Elisa had a strange dream: Her mother told her how she could release her brothers from the spell. She should knit shirts from stinging nettles and throw one over each of the swans. Until then, however, she was not allowed to speak a word, or else her brothers would die.
Elisa set to work immediately. Although her hands were burning as if they were on fire, she carried on knitting tirelessly.

Během dne labutě létaly pryč a v noci se všichni sourozenci tulili v jeskyni.

Jednu noc měla Elisa zvláštní sen: Její matka jí řekla, jak může své bratry vysvobodit. Měla každé labuti uplést košili z kopřiv a přehodit ji přes ni. Do té doby však nesměla prohodit ani slovíčko, jinak její bratři zemřou.
Elisa se dala ihned do práce. Ačkoliv ji ruce pálily jako oheň, neúnavně pletla dál.

One day hunting horns sounded in the distance. A prince came riding along with his entourage and he soon stood in front of her. As they looked into each other's eyes, they fell in love.

Jednoho dne se z dálky ozvaly lovecké rohy. Přijížděl princ s celou výpravou a brzy stál přímo před ní. Jakmile se sobě zadívali do očí, zamilovali se.

The prince lifted Elisa onto his horse and rode to his castle with her.

Princ vyzvedl Elisu na koně a dovezl ji do svého hradu.

The mighty treasurer was anything but pleased with the arrival of the silent beauty. His own daughter was meant to become the prince's bride.

Mocný správce pokladu nebyl z příjezdu němé krásky vůbec nadšený. Jeho vlastní dcera se totiž měla stát princovou nevěstou.

Elisa had not forgotten her brothers. Every evening she continued working on the shirts. One night she went out to the cemetery to gather fresh nettles. While doing so she was secretly watched by the treasurer.

Elisa ale nezapomněla na své bratry. Dál každý večer na košilích pracovala. Jednu noc šla na hřbitov sbírat čerstvé kopřivy. Správce pokladu ji tajně pozoroval.

As soon as the prince was away on a hunting trip, the treasurer had Elisa thrown into the dungeon. He claimed that she was a witch who met with other witches at night.

Hned jak jel princ na další hon, uvrhl správce Elisu do žaláře. Tvrdil, že je čarodějkou, co se v noci schází s jinými čarodějkami.

At dawn, Elisa was fetched by the guards. She was going to be burned to death at the marketplace.

Při úsvitu si pro Elisu přišla hradní stráž. Měla být upálena na tržišti.

No sooner had she arrived there, when suddenly eleven white swans came flying towards her. Elisa quickly threw a shirt over each of them. Shortly thereafter all her brothers stood before her in human form. Only the smallest, whose shirt had not been quite finished, still had a wing in place of one arm.

Sotva tam dorazila, přilétlo zničehonic jedenáct bílých labutí. Elisa přes každou rychle přehodila jednu košili. Krátce nato před ní stáli všichni její bratři v lidské podobě. Jen nejmladší bratr, jehož košile ještě nebyla dokončena, měl místo jedné paže křídlo.

The siblings' joyous hugging and kissing hadn't yet finished as the prince returned. At last Elisa could explain everything to him. The prince had the evil treasurer thrown into the dungeon. And after that the wedding was celebrated for seven days.

And they all lived happily ever after.

Objetí a polibky sourozenců ještě neutichly a princ byl již zpět. Konečně mu mohla Elisa vše vysvětlit. Princ nechal zlého správce uvalit do žaláře. A pak se sedm dní slavila svatba.

A všichni žili šťastně až do smrti.

Hans Christian Andersen

Hans Christian Andersen was born in the Danish city of Odense in 1805, and died in 1875 in Copenhagen. He gained world fame with his literary fairy-tales such as „The Little Mermaid", „The Emperor's New Clothes" and „The Ugly Duckling". The tale at hand, „The Wild Swans", was first published in 1838. It has been translated into more than one hundred languages and adapted for a wide range of media including theater, film and musical.

Barbara Brinkmann was born in Munich in 1969 and grew up in the foothills of the Bavarian Alps. She studied architecture in Munich and is currently a research associate in the Department of Architecture at the Technical University of Munich. She also works as a freelance graphic designer, illustrator, and author.

Cornelia Haas has been illustrating childrens' and adolescents' books since 2001. She was born near Augsburg, Germany, in 1972. She studied design at the Münster University of Applied Sciences and is currently a professor on the faculty of Münster University of Applied Sciences teaching illustration.

Marc Robitzky, born in 1973, studied at the Technical School of Art in Hamburg and the Academy of Visual Arts in Frankfurt. He works as a freelance illustrator and communication designer in Aschaffenburg (Germany).

Ulrich Renz was born in Stuttgart, Germany, in 1960. After studying French literature in Paris he graduated from medical school in Lübeck and worked as head of a scientific publishing company. He is now a writer of non-fiction books as well as children's fiction books.

Do you like drawing?

Here are the pictures from the story to color in:

www.sefa-bilingual.com/coloring

www.ingramcontent.com/pod-product-compliance
Lightning Source LLC
LaVergne TN
LVHW070448080526
838202LV00035B/2774